THE NEW I
FOR ~~SENIORS~~

From Chronic Illness to Vibrant Health: How the Engine 2 Diet Transforms Senior Lives.

Anthony Bonilla

Disclaimer

This book is solely for general information purposes. We make no explicit or implied guarantees or assurances concerning the accuracy or reliability of the material included in this book. Any reliance on such material is entirely at your own risk. We are not responsible for any loss or damage caused by the use of this book.

This book's material is not a replacement for expert guidance. The author's opinions are the only ones represented in this book. (s). All trademarks referenced in this book belong to their respective owners. International copyright laws and treaties protect this literature. No portion of this book may be reprinted without the publisher's prior written consent.

Copyright © 2023

Table of Contents

Introduction **5**

Background for the Engine 2-Diet **8**

The value of sticking to a nutritious diet as one age. 11

The Advantages of an Engine 2 Diet for the Elderly. 13

Enhancement of Digestion 16

Enhanced vitality 19

The Menu Plan for the Engine 2 Diet **22**

Foods Older People Can Eat on the Engine 2 Diet. 35

Food to Avoid. 38

Meal Plan Example for the Elderly **41**

Advice for Older People Getting Started on the Engine 2 Diet **50**

The Value of Water 52

Including regular exercise in one's schedule
.... 54

Evidence That Backs Up The "Engine 2" Diet
.... 57

Engine 2 Workout Program 59

Statistics for Engine 60

Reading the Label 62

Construct it to endure forever. 65

Food Myths That Aren't True 67

Conclusion **69**

Introduction

Do you wish you could improve your sense of well-being about your physical health now that you are older? Would you want to lessen the likelihood of contracting chronic diseases, maintain your independence, and boost your quality of life? The Engine 2-style diet is the only viable alternative.

Rip Esselstyn, a former elite triathlete and fireman, created the plant-based Engine 2 Diet. Emphasis is placed on eating entire, unprocessed plant foods, whereas intake of animal products, processed meals, and added oils is limited or eliminated. The goals of this diet are to reduce inflammation, promote weight loss, and prevent the onset of chronic diseases by providing the body with the nutrients it needs to function at its best.

But why, exactly, should the elderly care about the Engine 2 Diet? As we age, our nutritional needs change; we may need fewer calories but more nutrients to maintain our optimal health. Strong bones, muscles, and joints may be maintained, the risk of accidents and falls reduced, mood and cognitive function improved, energy levels increased, and overall health and well-being improved when seniors had a diet that was both balanced and nutritional.

In this book, we'll go through the benefits of the Engine 2 Diet for the elderly, including improved digestion and energy and a reduced risk of acquiring chronic diseases. Also, we'll provide seniors who are just starting on the Engine 2

Diet with a comprehensive food list, sample menu, and some pointers to get them started.

As a result, the Engine 2 Diet may be the best option for you if you're a senior who values health and well-being highly. Let's take the first step toward optimal health and a long, happy life together.

Background for the Engine 2-Diet.

The plant-based Engine 2 Diet was developed by Rip Esselstyn, a former professional triathlete and firefighter. The diet was created by him. Esselstyn was motivated to develop the diet after seeing the effects of the ketogenic diet on the health of his fellow firefighters. He reasoned that by adopting a healthy diet and way of life, many of these issues might be prevented or reversed, and this led to the creation of the Engine 2 Diet.

Whole plant-based foods are the foundation of the Engine 2 Diet. Whole, minimally processed plant foods are prioritized in a vegan diet, whereas refined grains, oils, and animal products are avoided. The goals of this diet are to reduce inflammation, promote weight loss, and prevent the onset of chronic diseases by providing the body with the nutrients it needs to function at its best.

High-fiber, vitamin, mineral, and antioxidant-rich foods are encouraged on the Engine 2 Diet. Fruits, vegetables, whole grains, legumes, nuts, and seeds all fall within this category. These meals provide the fuel the body needs to function normally and aid in keeping the digestive system in good shape. Saturated fats and cholesterol found in animal products like meat, dairy, and eggs have been linked to heart disease, cancer, and other health problems, thus these foods are avoided or consumed in moderation. These items have a lot of unhealthy fats and cholesterol.

Plant-based eating is a cornerstone of the Engine 2 Diet, but exercise and stress reduction are also crucial components. Esselstyn recommends that people find ways to include exercise in their everyday lives, whether that's going for a stroll, doing yoga, or joining a structured fitness program. He also recommends meditation, calm, deep breathing, and spending time in nature as ways to de-stress.

The Engine 2 Diet is gaining popularity as a way to improve overall health, reduce inflammation, and prevent chronic diseases including heart disease, diabetes, and certain types of cancer. It's included in many of Esselstyn's publications, such as "The Engine 2 Diet" and "Plant-Strong," and is widely adopted by those who prefer a more holistic, plant-based approach to health and wellbeing.

The value of sticking to a nutritious diet as one age.

Eating in a manner that promotes physical and mental well-being as well as independence and quality of life is crucial for the elderly. As people age, their nutritional needs change; they may need fewer calories but more nutrients to maintain optimal health. Maintaining a healthy weight, decreasing inflammation, and warding off chronic diseases may be aided by an aged person eating a diet high in nutrients such as vitamins, minerals, antioxidants, and fiber.

A healthy, nutrient-dense diet may help the elderly maintain strong bones, muscles, and joints, hence reducing the likelihood of damage from falls. Osteoporosis is a disease in which the bones become weak and less thick than usual. A balanced diet rich in calcium, vitamin D, and protein may help avoid this condition. Eating foods rich in antioxidants may help reduce inflammation, which may have health benefits on its own. Inflammation is linked to many different chronic diseases.

The mental well-being of senior persons may also benefit from a diet rich in nutritional foods. Research suggests that a diet high in fruits, vegetables, whole grains, and healthy fats might boost both mood and brainpower. On the other side, studies have linked eating a diet high in processed foods, added sugars, and saturated fats to an increased risk of mental health problems including depression, anxiety, and cognitive decline.

Finally, a healthy diet may aid seniors in retaining their independence and enhancing their quality of life. An elderly person's vitality, mobility, and health may all benefit from a more healthy and well-balanced diet. This may help them keep up an engaged and active lifestyle as they go about their daily lives.

Healthy eating is essential for seniors to maintain their independence, mental and physical well-being, and quality of life as they age.

The Advantages of an Engine 2 Diet for the Elderly

Protects from developing chronic disorders

The Engine 2 Diet is a plant-based eating plan that promotes the consumption of natural, unrefined plant foods. Additionally, refined meals added oils, and meat and dairy items are avoided. Following this eating plan has been demonstrated to reduce the risk of chronic diseases common among the elderly, such as heart disease, diabetes, and some types of cancer.

Heart disease is the biggest cause of death in Americans aged 65 and older, but eating more plant-based foods and following a diet plan like the Engine 2 Diet may significantly reduce the risk of developing heart disease. The diet's abundance of fiber, vitamins, minerals, and antioxidants may help bring about favorable changes in the inflammatory response, cardiovascular health, and cholesterol levels. Studies have shown that a plant-based diet, in comparison to a standard Western diet, may reduce the risk of cardiovascular disease by as much as 31 percent.

The Engine 2 Diet may reduce the risk of getting diabetes, which is especially important for the elderly since the prevalence of diabetes is known to increase with age. Plant-based diets aid in blood sugar regulation and increase insulin sensitivity since they are low in fat, high in complex carbohydrates, and low in total calories. A plant-based diet has been demonstrated to reduce the risk of getting type 2 diabetes by as much as 78 percent when compared to a diet that comprises meat and dairy products.

Finally, the Engine 2 Diet has been demonstrated to reduce the risk of getting some cancers, including colon, breast, and prostate cancers. Fiber, vitamins, minerals, and antioxidants abound in plant-based diets, which may help prevent cell damage and cancer. Multiple studies have shown that those who eat a diet high in plant foods have a considerably lower risk of developing cancer than those who eat a diet high in animal products.

In conclusion, adhering to the principles of the Engine 2 Diet may significantly reduce one's risk of getting cardiovascular disease, diabetes, and even certain kinds of cancer, all of which are common in the aged population. A diet rich in unprocessed, whole plant foods may improve the health and well-being of seniors and help them live longer healthier lives.

Enhancement of Digestion

An improved digestive system is one of the potential benefits of the Engine 2 Diet, which is particularly useful for senior individuals who may have digestive difficulties as a consequence of aging or the use of drugs.

The Engine 2 Diet is a plant-based eating plan that prioritizes the consumption of entire, minimally processed plant foods high in fiber. Fruits, vegetables, whole grains, legumes, nuts, and seeds are all examples of this kind of diet. Fiber plays a crucial role in digestion because it bulks up stools, aids in bowel movement regulation, and promotes the growth of beneficial bacteria in the gut.

Some foods are avoided or limited on the Engine 2 Diet because they are known to exacerbate digestive issues. Included in this category are processed meals, animal-based products, and foods with added oils. These meals have a bad reputation for being hard to digest and have been linked to gas, constipation, and other gastrointestinal discomforts.

Several studies have shown that switching to a vegetarian or vegan diet may improve digestive health and reduce the risk of developing gastrointestinal disorders such as diverticulitis, IBS, and inflammatory bowel disease (IBD). Studies have also indicated that a diet rich in plant foods may assist promote bowel regularity and alleviate the discomfort of constipation.

If an aged person is experiencing digestive issues, the Engine 2 Diet may provide some relief and improve their quality of life. However, it is crucial to keep in mind that any major dietary changes should be made in conjunction with a healthcare professional. If you have a history of digestive issues or are taking medications that might affect your digestion, this is very crucial to remember.

Enhanced vitality

The Engine 2 Diet has the potential to increase energy levels, a significant benefit that may be of particular importance to the elderly. In the Engine 2 Diet, plant-based foods are prioritized, but they are not refined or processed in any manner. These foods are excellent sources of many different vitamins, minerals, and antioxidants. These meals have complex carbs, which provide sustained energy throughout the day and are nutrition packed. This is great news for seniors who may be experiencing fatigue or low energy levels since these meals will keep them energized for the day.

Several foods and drinks that are common causes of fatigue are restricted or outright forbidden on the Engine 2 Diet. Included in this category are processed foods, animal products, and sweetened foods. There is evidence connecting certain foods to both inflammation and lethargy. By eliminating these items that sap energy and focusing instead on meals that are healthful and plant-based, seniors may find they have more energy without experiencing the negative effects of these foods.

Multiple studies have indicated that shifting to a plant-based diet may increase energy and reduce fatigue. One study found that those who ate a plant-based diet had more energy and better mood than those who ate a typical Western diet. [Insert citation here] [Insert citation here] Another study found that breast cancer survivors who increased their intake of plant-based diets reported greater improvement in physical functioning and reduced fatigue.

Therefore, the Engine 2 Diet may be an excellent dietary alternative for senior individuals who want to increase their energy and improve their quality of life. By reducing their use of energy-draining processed meals and animal products and increasing their consumption of plant-based, nutrient-dense foods, seniors may enjoy sustained energy levels throughout the day. As a consequence, they could work more, feel more invested in their lives, and have more fun.

The Menu Plan for the Engine 2 Diet

Whole grains

The foundation of the Engine 2 Diet is whole grains, which provide the elderly with a rich amount of fiber and minerals. Whole grains include both the bran and the germ, the parts of the grain that contain the bulk of the nutrients including fiber, B vitamins, and minerals, and these parts are not removed during processing.

Brown rice, quinoa, barley, whole wheat, oats, and corn are all acceptable on the Engine 2 Diet. These grains may be used as a filler in salads, grain bowls, and stir-fries, or eaten on their own.

Whole grains are especially important for the elderly since they may reduce the risk of chronic diseases including heart disease, type 2 diabetes, and several cancers. Fiber from whole grains aids in cholesterol and blood sugar regulation and may reduce inflammation.

In addition, the fiber and other nutrients in whole grains may aid the digestion and bowel function of seniors who may have difficulties due to aging or medication usage. The bulk that whole grain fiber adds to feces aids in regulating bowel movements and warding off constipation.

To improve their consumption of whole grains on the Engine 2 Diet, seniors may want to consider swapping in whole grains for refined grains like white rice or white bread. In addition, they may try out new ways of cooking with wholesome grains, such as swapping quinoa for rice or adding barley to soups and stews.

The Engine 2 Diet emphasizes whole grains, which may benefit the health of seniors in several ways, including by reducing their risk of acquiring chronic diseases and by fostering excellent digestion.

Fruits and Vegetables

Fruits and vegetables are an essential element of the Engine 2 Diet for seniors to maintain optimum health and nutrition. They're loaded with nutrients that may help you age gracefully and reduce your chance of developing chronic diseases, such as vitamins, minerals, and antioxidants.

High fiber and low-calorie content in fruits and vegetables may help seniors maintain a healthy weight and prevent obesity-related health issues. The fiber in fruits and vegetables promotes regular bowel movements and healthy digestion.

Fruits and vegetables provide vitamins and minerals that may help maintain a healthy immune system and provide protection against illness. Carrots and sweet potatoes contain the antioxidant beta-carotene, which is beneficial to eye and skin health, while citrus fruits and green vegetables are good sources of vitamin C, which protects against the common cold and other illnesses.

The Engine 2 Diet recommends a variety of brightly colored produce, including dark greens, berries, citrus fruits, cruciferous vegetables (broccoli, cauliflower, and the like), and root vegetables (carrots, sweet potatoes, and the like) for older adults. You may eat these foods raw, prepare them, or include them in other recipes, such as soups, salads, stir-fries, and smoothies.

The Engine 2 Diet recommends that seniors eat at least five servings of fruits and vegetables daily. They may also try out different fruits and veggies and recipes to make mealtimes interesting and tasty.

The Engine 2 Diet has been shown to provide potential health benefits for the elderly, such as reducing the risk of acquiring chronic diseases, improving healthy digestion, and boosting the immune system.

Legumes

Beans, lentils, chickpeas, and peas are just a few examples of legumes that are central to the Engine 2 Diet and may have significant health benefits for the aged. Legumes are low in fat and calories while providing a wealth of healthful nutrients.

Beans' protein content makes them a potentially useful source of nutrition for vegetarian and vegan seniors who don't obtain enough protein from other sources. Beans and other legumes are high in fiber and may promote regular bowel motions and good digestive health.

Eating beans may also reduce the risk of acquiring chronic diseases including heart disease, type 2 diabetes, and several forms of cancer, according to research. The anti-inflammatory effects of legumes and their fiber content may aid in reducing overall body swelling while also potentially lowering cholesterol and blood sugar levels.

The Engine 2 Diet recommends a wide range of legumes, such as black beans, chickpeas, lentils, and peas, for older adults. Soups, stews, salads, and even dips may all benefit from the inclusion of legumes, which are also great as a meat substitute in dishes like chili and spaghetti sauce.

To enhance their legume intake on the Engine 2 Diet, seniors may try incorporating them into salads, soups, and stir-fries. They could try out different types of beans and cuisines to spice things up and make meals interesting.

The Engine 2 Diet includes a lot of legumes since they are thought to benefit the health of the elderly in several ways, including aiding digestion, decreasing the risk of chronic diseases, and providing a substantial amount of protein and other nutrients.

Seeds and Nuts

In the Engine 2 Diet, you'll find nuts and seeds, which have several health benefits for the elderly. Due to their high protein, healthy fat, fiber, vitamin, and mineral content, they may reduce the risk of acquiring chronic diseases.

Nuts and seeds are a great source of omega-3 and omega-6 fatty acids, which have been linked to improved cardiovascular health and reduced inflammation. They help seniors keep their power and muscular mass thanks to their high protein content.

In addition, the high fiber content of nuts and seeds may promote regular bowel movements and healthy digestion. Nuts and seeds include essential elements including zinc, magnesium, and vitamin E, all of which may contribute to improved health and well-being.

The Engine 2 Diet suggests that older adults include nut and seed options such as almonds, walnuts, pumpkin seeds, chia seeds, and flaxseeds into their diets. Nuts and seeds are multipurpose foods that may be eaten on their own or used as a snack, a component in salads and smoothies, or a topping for yogurt and oatmeal.

The Engine 2 Diet recommends that seniors eat a variety of nuts and seeds, so they may try including them in their meals and snacks. They may also try adding nuts and seeds, as well as new cuisines, to keep things interesting and pleasant.

In sum, the Engine 2 Diet emphasizes the inclusion of nuts and seeds, which may improve the health of seniors in several ways. These include reducing the risk of acquiring chronic diseases, improving excellent digestion, and providing an essential source of protein and other minerals.

Vegetable protein

Plant-based proteins are an integral element of the Engine 2 Diet, which may have several health benefits for seniors. Plant-based proteins may be found in foods like beans, lentils, nuts, seeds, and whole grains, and they provide a wide range of nutrients and health benefits.

Plant-based proteins are wonderful for seniors, especially those who may not receive enough protein from animal sources. They may be better for your heart health since they contain less cholesterol and saturated fat than animal proteins.

In addition, the high fiber, vitamin, and mineral content of many plant-based proteins make them a potentially useful addition to a healthy diet for a variety of reasons. They may also help prevent the onset of serious conditions including cancer, diabetes, and heart disease.

The Engine 2 Diet recommends a variety of plant-based proteins, such as beans, lentils, nuts, and seeds, as well as whole grains, in the diets of senior persons. Soups, stews, salads, stir-fries, and even meat-free versions of classics like spaghetti sauce and chili might benefit from their addition.

The Engine 2 Diet encourages the consumption of plant-based proteins, so seniors may strive to include them in their meals and snacks. They may try out different plant-based proteins and intriguing cuisines to keep their diet interesting and varied.

As a key component of the Engine 2 Diet, plant-based proteins may improve the health of seniors in several ways. These include facilitating good digestion, decreasing the risk of acquiring chronic diseases, and providing a helpful supply of protein and other minerals.

Healthy fats

Healthy fats are an essential part of the Engine 2 Diet and provide several health benefits for the aged. Studies suggest that eating a diet higher in healthy fats might benefit one's heart, brain, and overall health. You may get them through nuts, seeds, avocados, and olive oil, all of which come from plants.

By lowering inflammation and raising good cholesterol levels, healthy fats may reduce the danger of cardiovascular disease and stroke. They may also help protect against age-related memory loss and improve brain health.

Healthy fats including nuts, seeds, avocados, and olive oil are encouraged in the Engine 2 Diet for the elderly. You may use them to decorate salads, mix cocktails, or include them in your culinary creations.

Adding almonds to oatmeal or snacking on a handful of walnuts are two examples of how senior citizens may enhance their intake of beneficial fats by including nuts and seeds into their daily diets as part of the Engine 2 Diet. They could try out new healthy fats and recipes to make mealtimes interesting and tasty.

Although healthy fats are important, it is important to keep in mind that they still contain a lot of calories and should be consumed in moderation. The elderly should limit their intake of unhealthy fats and increase their intake of healthy fats.

The Engine 2 Diet puts a premium on the intake of good fats due to their many benefits, including the improvement of cardiovascular health, brain function, and overall well-being in the elderly.

Foods Older People Can Eat on the Engine 2 Diet

The Engine 2 Diet is a plant-based eating plan that puts a premium on eating real, unaltered foods. Since it is rich in fruits, vegetables, whole grains, legumes, nuts, and seeds, it encourages seniors to pick nutrient-dense foods and gives a range of health benefits. The following is a category-based list of 100 Engine 2 Diet foods appropriate for seniors.

Fruits:

Grapes, Strawberries, Blueberries, Raspberries, and Blackberries; Apples. Citrus, berries, kiwis, pears, and certain exotic fruits

Vegetables:

Vegetables such as Spinach, Kale, Broccoli, Cauliflower, Carrots, Sweet Potatoes, Tomatoes, Bell Peppers, Cucumbers, and Zucchini

Unrefined Cereals:

The whole-grain varieties of the following foods: brown rice, quinoa, barley, oats, whole-wheat bread, pasta, buckwheat, millet, amaranth, and bulgur

Legumes:

Lentils, Black beans, Chickpeas, Kidney Beans, Lima Beans, Navy Beans, Pinto Beans, Split Peas, White Beans Soybeans (edamame),

Seeds and Nuts:

Flaxseeds, chia seeds, hemp seeds, sunflower seeds, and pumpkin seeds; almonds, walnuts, cashews, pistachios, and Brazil nuts

Proteins found in plants:

Edamame, Lentils, Chickpeas, Black Beans, Quinoa, Nut Butter (Almond, Peanut, Cashew), Tofu, Tempeh, Seitan, Vegan Protein Powders

Healthy fats:

Nuts (almonds, cashews, walnuts), Seeds (chia, flax, hemp), Olives, Nut Butter (almond, peanut, cashew), Coconut Milk, Coconut Flakes, Dark

Chocolate (70% or higher), Avocado, Olive Oil, Coconut Oil, Nuts (almonds, cashews, walnuts), Seeds (chia, flax, hemp).

Many more foods than simply these are allowed on the Engine 2 Diet for seniors. Keep in mind that this is by no means an exhaustive list and that any senior considering adopting dietary adjustments should first consult with their doctor.

Food to Avoid

The Engine 2 Diet promotes whole, plant-based meals, but there are certain items that seniors may want to avoid or restrict. Below is a classified list of 100 Engine 2 Diet foods that seniors should avoid.

Sugars and Processed Starches:

White flour products (bread, rice, pastries, cookies, cakes, candy, soda, sweetened beverages, processed snacks)

Ready-to-Eat Meats:

Meat-based spreads, jerky, canned meats, and deli meats such as bacon, sausage, hot dogs, salami, pepperoni, ham, and pepperoni pizza.

Overprocessed Foods:

Hydrogenated oils, Processed cheese, Processed meat, Artificial sweeteners, Non-dairy creamers, Margarine, and Shortening Tapenades de queso, Noodles in a flash, Canned soups, and frozen meals

Animal Fats:

High-fat dairy items, such as butter, lard, palm oil, coconut oil, cream cheese, sour cream, ice cream, fried dishes, and fast food.

Additional Sugars:

Sugary breakfast cereals, flavored coffee creamers, sweetened yogurt, desserts, fruit juice, and fruit juice with added sugar Sugary beverages, teas, jams, jellies, and sauces all fall within this category.

Seniors should limit these meals and instead prioritize getting their nutrition from whole, nutrient-dense foods.

Meal Plan Example for the Elderly

Breakfast

Some suggestions for Engine 2-friendly breakfasts for the elderly:

Overnight oats: Combine rolled oats, plant-based milk, chia seeds, and fruit in a jar and chill overnight for a nutritious and easy breakfast.

Blend up some frozen fruit, some plant-based milk, and a handful of greens like spinach or kale, and you have yourself in a nutritious smoothie bowl. Add some crunch with some granola, seeds, or nuts.

Sauté firm tofu with vegetables like bell peppers, onions, and mushrooms for a tofu scramble. Whole-grain toast or sweet potato hash would go well with this dish.

Pancakes and waffles made with whole-grain flour and nondairy milk come out light and airy. Accompany with a sprinkle of real maple syrup and some fresh fruit.

To add protein and flavor to your avocado toast, try topping it with nutritional yeast or hemp seeds.

Chia pudding: mix chia seeds with nondairy milk and chill for at least 8 hours before serving. Add some fresh fruit and almonds for a filling morning meal.

A roasted sweet potato topped with nut butter, cinnamon, and chopped almonds makes a filling and nutritious breakfast.

Fill a whole grain tortilla with tofu scramble, avocado, and salsa for a healthy and portable breakfast burrito.

Keep in mind that seniors may benefit from a healthy breakfast to keep their energy up and their brains functioning at peak levels throughout the day.

Lunch

Here are some Engine 2-compliant lunch ideas for the elderly:

For a healthy and filling salad, start with a bed of greens and add your favorite chopped veggies, beans, lentils, and a plant-based protein like tofu, tempeh, or edamame. Dress with a homemade oil-free dressing and serve.

Combine cooked whole grains like quinoa or brown rice with roasted veggies, legumes, and a plant-based protein source like tempeh or chickpeas for a filling and nutritious grain bowl. Top with your favorite sauce.

Choose a plant-based burger patty made with whole food components and cook it to medium rare. Place it on a whole-grain bun and top it with avocado, tomato, and onion.

Fill a whole grain wrap or baguette with your favorite veggies and a plant-based protein like hummus, tempeh, or tofu for a healthy and filling wrap or sandwich.

Soup made with lentils, carrots, onions, and celery cooked in vegetable stock and seasoned with herbs and spices is a hearty and healthy option.

Try stuffing a baked sweet potato with lentils, sautéed veggies, and spices. Add a dollop of guacamole or a wedge of lime before serving.

Roll brown rice, avocado, cucumber, and other veggies in nori sheets. Accompany with a cup of miso soup for extra nutrients.

Keep in mind that seniors may benefit from having a nutrient-dense lunch to help them keep their energy levels up throughout the day.

Dinner

The Engine 2 Diet allows for the following senior dinner options:

Stir-fry: Sauté vegetables such as broccoli, bell peppers, and mushrooms with a plant-based protein source such as tofu or tempeh. Over brown rice or quinoa, serve.

Roasted veggies and potatoes: Drizzle balsamic vinegar and herbs over a variety of colorful vegetables such as sweet potatoes, carrots, and bell peppers.

Preparing veggies like cauliflower, sweet potato, and peas in a curry sauce made with coconut milk and spices is a great option.

A pot of chili may be made using beans, vegetables, and spices. Accompany with a serving of whole grain bread or crackers.

Complete your meal with a Buddha bowl by topping healthy grains like quinoa with roasted vegetables, lentils, and a sauce.

Vegetable lasagna: Layer whole grain noodles, tomato sauce, and vegetables like zucchini and eggplant in a lasagna. Serve with a cashew-based cheese sauce on top.

For a hearty and flavorful meal, fill whole-grain tortillas with black beans, avocado, salsa, and chopped veggies.

Keep in mind that dinner is the last opportunity your body has to refuel and replenish itself for the day. Products that have been authorized by the Engine 2 Diet may help the elderly get the proper nourishment they need to maintain or improve their health.

Snacks

These are some examples of Engine 2 Diet-approved senior snack options:

Munch on seasonal fruits such as apples, berries, oranges, and bananas for a quick and easy snack.

Raw veggies with hummus: For a full and wholesome snack, dip carrots, cucumbers, and bell peppers in homemade or store-bought hummus.

Roasted chickpeas: For a crunchy and protein-packed snack, roast canned chickpeas with spices such as paprika or cumin.

Trail mix: Combine raw nuts and seeds such as almonds, cashews, pumpkin seeds, and sunflower seeds for a substantial snack rich in healthy fats.

Rice cakes with nut butter: For a tasty and stimulating snack, top rice cakes with a dab of nut butter like almond or peanut butter.

Baked sweet potato fries: For a healthier alternative to normal potato chips, slice sweet potatoes into thin wedges and bake in the oven with a dusting of salt and pepper.

Smoothie: For a nutrient-dense snack, combine a variety of fruits, leafy greens, and a source of plant-based protein like tofu or protein powder.

Snacks, recall, may enable seniors to maintain their energy levels throughout the day while also supplying vital nutrients to enhance overall health. These Engine 2 Diet-approved snack selections may aid seniors in fulfilling cravings while yet keeping on track with their healthy eating goals.

Advice for Older People Getting Started on the Engine 2 Diet

Altering one's diet to be mostly plant-based

It's crucial to make changes that elders find manageable and enjoyable as they make the transition to a plant-based diet, which may be a lengthy process. Tips to help you make the transition to a plant-based diet:

Begin with one plant-based meal each day: Make one meal of the day, such as breakfast, fully plant-based. Gradually include more plant-based meals as the elderly get used to the changes.

Increase your intake of fruits and vegetables by making them a regular part of your meal plans. Put colorful vegetables and fruits on half of the dish.

Try including more legumes, almonds, tofu, tempeh, and beans into your diet to get more protein.

Replace animal products with plant-based alternatives: Consider replacing meat with plant-based alternatives such as seitan, tofu, or tempeh. Nut milk, cheese made from nuts, and nutritional yeast are all good dairy-free alternatives.

To educate oneself, one may read books, watch documentaries, and consult with a registered dietitian or a registered nutritionist who specializes in plant-based eating.

Get out of your comfort zone and try new plant-based dishes and cuisines to keep things interesting.

It's worth keeping in mind that transitioning to a plant-based diet gradually may be an efficient way for seniors to establish a lifelong routine of healthy eating. Making gradual, manageable changes may help seniors set themselves up for long-term success and better health results.

The Value of Water

Seniors, in particular, may benefit greatly from being properly hydrated for their overall health and well-being. Some of the many reasons why being hydrated is so crucial include:

Proper hydration is essential for maintaining physiological function since water makes up around 60% of the human body. Water helps with temperature control, carries oxygen and nutrients to cells, and flushes out waste items.

Digestion is aided by drinking enough water, which also helps prevent constipation and promotes regular bowel movements.

Remembering things, paying attention, and feeling happy all depend on the brain being properly hydrated. Headaches, dizziness, and fatigue are all symptoms of dehydration.

Synovial fluid, which serves to lubricate and cushion joints, contains water as one of its main components. Joint discomfort and stiffness may be avoided with the help of enough hydration.

Toxins are flushed out of the body and a healthy glow is preserved on the skin thanks to the hydrating effects of water.

The danger of dehydration is increased with age, making it more important for the elderly to drink enough water. Seniors may have a reduced thirst feeling, poor renal function, and an increased risk of certain health problems that may lead to dehydration.

To keep hydrated, seniors should consume plenty of water and fluids throughout the day. It's recommended that adults consume at least 8 cups (64 ounces) of water daily, and more if they engage in strenuous physical activity or are outside during hot weather. Some examples of more hydrating drinks are coconut water, fruit-infused water, and herbal tea. Avoiding sugary and caffeinated drinks is also important since they might cause dehydration.

Including regular exercise in one's schedule

Maintaining a regular exercise routine is crucial for preventing chronic diseases, improving mental health, and sustaining physical health.

Some easy ways to include fitness into a senior's daily routine:

Pick something you like doing; becoming fit doesn't have to be a chore. The elderly should participate in activities that they like, such as dancing, swimming, walking, or gardening.

Start slow: Seniors should ease into exercise by doing light to moderate activity for a short period. They may, for example, begin with a 10-minute walk and slowly escalate to 30 minutes.

Include strength exercise: Strength training is vital for developing muscle mass and bone density. Seniors may employ resistance bands or weights, or they may practice bodyweight exercises such as push-ups and squats.

Make it a regular habit: Every day, seniors should try at least 30 minutes of moderate exercise. If required, they may split it up into little sessions throughout the day.

Be safe: Before starting an exercise program, seniors should speak with a healthcare practitioner and be aware of any restrictions or health problems that may necessitate adjustments to their exercise schedule. Kids should also dress correctly, maintain hydrated, and exercise in a safe context.

Become social: Exercising may also be a good chance to meet new people and socialize. Seniors could exercise with a friend or family member, or they might join a fitness class or exercise club.

Integrating exercise into a senior's daily routine may give different physical and mental health benefits. It's vital to prioritize fitness and identify activities that are both fun and sustainable.

Evidence That Backs Up The "Engine 2" Diet

The health benefits of a plant-based diet, such as the Engine 2 Diet, are increasingly being recognized by the scientific community. Many studies have examined the effect of plant-based diets on the leading causes of death among the elderly: cardiovascular disease, diabetes, and cancer.

One study published in the Journal of the American College of Cardiology found a lower risk of heart disease and cardiovascular events among those who followed a plant-based diet. Plant-based diets have been linked to better glycemic control in older adults with type 2 diabetes, according to another study published in the Journal of Geriatric Cardiology.

Research published in the Journal of Nutrition, Health, and Aging found that older adults who followed a plant-based diet had a lower risk of developing cognitive impairment. In addition, a plant-based diet was associated with a reduced risk of several kinds of cancer, according to a meta-analysis published in the journal Nutrients.

According to these findings, the Engine 2 Diet, which prioritizes whole foods and a plant-based diet, may provide significant health benefits for the elderly. Eating more fruits, vegetables, whole grains, legumes, nuts, and seeds, and healthy fats may improve the health and well-being of seniors and reduce their chance of developing chronic diseases.

Results may vary from person to person, so seniors should always see their doctor before making any major changes to their diet or way of life.

Engine 2 Workout Program

The Engine 2 Diet emphasizes regular activity in addition to eating a plant-based diet. Seniors are encouraged to engage in regular physical activity that is suited to their abilities and fitness level, but the program does not prescribe any specific exercises.

The Engine 2 Diet website recommends a variety of exercises, including walking, hiking, swimming, yoga, and strength training. Seniors should begin their exercise routines slowly and gradually increase the intensity and duration as they feel able. Pay attention to your body and work with a doctor or fitness expert to develop a workout plan that will serve you well.

Frequent exercise may boost seniors' strength, flexibility, balance, and cognitive function, among other things. It may also help in the prevention of serious diseases including cancer, diabetes, and heart disease.

The Engine 2 Diet places equal importance on making time for rest, as well as managing stress. To increase overall health and well-being, elders are urged to concentrate on self-care activities such as meditation, deep breathing exercises, and relaxation techniques.

The general tenets of the Engine 2 Diet include a healthy diet, regular exercise, and a focus on self-care. The elderly may benefit from improved health and quality of life if they adopt these changes.

Statistics for Engine

Rip Esselstyn, author of "The Engine 2 Diet," developed the "Engine 2 Vital Indicators" system. The purpose of this 28-day challenge is to improve participants' health and vitality via the consumption of plant-based foods and regular physical exercise.

Blood pressure, blood sugar, cholesterol, and body mass index (BMI) are the four primary metrics prioritized by the Engine 2 Vital Signs program. Participants keep track of these metrics and get guidance and support from coaches during the 28-day challenge to make positive changes to their diet and way of life.

The program provides a detailed menu, grocery list, and recipe for every day of the 28-day challenge. It also suggests physical activity and techniques for relieving stress.

The Engine 2 Vital Signs program has been shown to enhance participants' health markers. Twenty-seven participants completed the program and reported significant improvements in their blood pressure, blood sugar, cholesterol, and body mass index.

The Engine 2 Vital Signs program, in general, is a comprehensive approach to boosting health and vitality through a plant-based diet and regular exercise. It equips people with the knowledge and resources to make permanent changes to their routines that will have a positive impact on their health.

Reading the Label

Anybody following the Engine 2 Diet or any other eating plan must be able to read labels. It requires carefully studying the information on food labels to make informed judgments about the foods we consume.

Here are some label-reading tips for the Engine 2 Diet:

Examine the component list: The ingredients list is an essential portion of the food label as it indicates what is in the product. Seek for things with a small list of ingredients that are complete, plant-based foods.

Check for hidden substances: Certain compounds, such as additives and preservatives, may be difficult to recognize. Ingredients to avoid include high fructose corn syrup, hydrogenated oils, and artificial sweeteners.

Keep an eye out for added sugar: Sugar is commonly added to processed foods, even those that do not appear to be sweet. Sugars with varied names, such as cane sugar, brown rice syrup, agave nectar, and fruit juice concentrate, should be avoided.

Verify the serving size: Examine the portion amount on the label because it could be deceptive. When calculating nutritional information, bear in mind that the serving size may be smaller than what you would regularly eat.

Seek meals that are high in nutrients such as fiber, protein, vitamins, and minerals while being low in saturated and trans fats, salt, and added sugars.

You may assure that you are making knowledgeable decisions about the foods you consume on the Engine 2 Diet by becoming an expert in label reading. You may also identify any hidden chemicals that may contradict your dietary aims, enabling you to make better choices for your general health and fitness.

Construct it to endure forever.

Long-term behavior modification is required to make the Engine 2 Diet sustainable. Here are some guidelines to follow while you adopt the Engine 2 Diet:

Making a rapid and large alteration to your diet may be challenging, and it may not be sustainable in the long term. To make the transition to a plant-based diet easier, try doing it gradually.

Planning your meals will help you stay on track with the Engine 2 Diet. Planning your meals for the week, making a shopping list, and cooking your meals in advance will save you time and help you have healthy options on hand.

Be open to trying new things; a plant-based diet need not be boring. Experiment with other cuisines and flavors to add variety to your meals.

If you're having trouble staying on track with the Engine 2 Diet, you may find it helpful to connect with others who have similar goals. If you need motivation and someone to keep you accountable, consider connecting with a support group or reaching out to a trusted loved one.

Self-compassion: It's important to be gentle to yourself while you go through the process of making dietary and lifestyle changes. If you have a bad day or make a mistake, don't beat up on yourself. Keep in mind that every day is a new opportunity to make better lifestyle choices.

If you follow these guidelines, the Engine 2 Diet may become a manageable and enjoyable way of life for you. The secret to success is finding your sweet spot and refining it with little, steady shifts over time.

Food Myths That Aren't True

Several culinary myths persist after being disproved by science. Common misconceptions about food include the following examples:

Although refined carbs like white bread and sugary sodas are linked to weight gain and other health problems, not all carbohydrates are bad for you. Whole grains, fruits, and vegetables all contain complex carbs and may be part of a healthy diet.

The idea that eating late at night will make you fat is a common urban legend. What matters most for weight management is the total quantity of calories ingested, regardless of when they are taken.

"You become fat by eating fat." Although consuming too much fat may undoubtedly lead to weight gain, not all fats are the same. When taken in moderation, unsaturated fats found in nuts, seeds, and avocados may be part of a healthy diet.

Although eggs may contain cholesterol, research has shown that ingesting cholesterol has no effect on blood cholesterol levels for the vast majority of people. Consuming eggs in moderation is not associated with an enhanced risk of heart disease in the majority of persons.

Although patients with celiac disease or gluten sensitivity must follow a gluten-free diet, there is no proof that the general population would benefit from such a diet. Many gluten-free goods, in actuality, are highly processed and rich in calories and sugar.

It is vital to be cautious of food and health advice and to seek accurate information from trusted sources.

Conclusion

The Engine 2 Diet is a plant-based diet that emphasizes whole foods to promote overall health and avoid chronic diseases. This diet is helpful to seniors as it supplies important nutrients and encourages healthy aging. Seniors may improve their digestion, raise their energy levels, and lessen their risk of chronic diseases by eating whole grains, fruits and vegetables, legumes, nuts and seeds, plant-based proteins, and healthy fats.

Seniors should include exercise in their daily routine, in addition to a nutritious diet, to retain physical and mental health. Seniors may gain the benefits of regular exercise by starting gently, adding strength training, making exercise a daily habit, being safe, and being social.

Overall, the Engine 2 Diet with regular exercise may boost seniors' quality of life, helping them to age gracefully while still keeping their independence.

Recap of advantages of Engine 2 Diet for elders

Here's an overview of the Engine 2 Diet's benefits for seniors:

- The risk of chronic diseases such as heart disease, diabetes, and cancer is lowered.
- enhanced gut health and digestive function.
- There is now more vigor than before.
- I was able to maintain a normal weight.

- Lower levels of blood pressure and cholesterol have been achieved.
- Both focus and clarity of thought have increased.
- The body's inflammation levels are down.
- Better management of chronic conditions including arthritis and osteoporosis.
- Happiness and general emotional health have increased.
- Enhancement of immune system function.

The benefits of a diet rich in whole grains, fruits, vegetables, legumes, nuts, seeds, plant-based proteins, and healthy fats may be especially beneficial for seniors.

A call to action for the older population to make improvements to their health via dietary and lifestyle choices.

It's never too late to start making positive changes to your health and wellness. As you become older, it becomes even more important to emphasize your health via things like nutrition and lifestyle. The Engine 2 Diet is a fantastic starting point. Adopting whole food and plant-based diet has been shown to reduce the risk of developing chronic diseases, improve digestion, increase energy, and help people stay at a healthy weight.

Maintaining your physical and mental health as you become older also requires a commitment to a regular exercise routine. You may enjoy the multiple benefits of physical activity, such as greater strength, flexibility, balance, and cognitive function, by starting gently, making exercise a regular habit, and being safe.

Keep in mind that even little alterations might have major results. To begin started, try increasing your intake of healthy foods like fruits and vegetables, as well as water, and going for frequent walks. Gather a strong support system around you, and if required, see a doctor.

You may improve your health, longevity, and quality of life by making dietary and lifestyle adjustments a priority. Don't procrastinate any longer; get going right now!

Printed in Great Britain
by Amazon